AMY BARTH

101 TIPS

FOR SURVIVORS OF SEXUAL ABUSE

A POCKET BOOK OF WISDOM

101 Tips For Survivors of Sexual Abuse: A Pocket Book of Wisdom
Copyright © 2009 by Amy Barth. All Rights Reserved.
Author info at www.AmyJBarth.com

No part of this publication may be reproduced, transmitted in any form or by any means, electronic, mechanical, photocopying, recording, or otherwise, or stored in a retrieval system, without the prior written consent of the publisher.

Library of Congress Cataloging-in-Publication Data
Barth, Amy, 1959-
  101 tips for survivors of sexual abuse : a pocket book of wisdom / by Amy Barth.
     p. cm.
  Includes bibliographical references.
  ISBN-13: 978-1-932690-94-1 (trade paper : alk. paper)
  ISBN-10: 1-932690-94-8 (trade paper : alk. paper)
 1. Sexual abuse victims--Psychology. 2. Adult child abuse victims--Psychology. I. Title. II. Title: One hundred and one tips for survivors of sexual abuse.
  HV6556.B377 2009
  616.85'8369--dc22
                                                  2009017490

Published by Loving Healing Press
5145 Pontiac Trail
Ann Arbor, MI 48105
Tollfree 888-761-6268
Fax 734-663-6861

www.LovingHealing.com
info@LovingHealing.com

Contents

Preface	iii
Foreword	iv
How to Use this Book	v
101 Tips	1
Things to do when having a "bad moment"	21
Exercises to strengthen your core	21
Bibliography / Suggested Reading	23
About the Author	24

~For~

To the girls and young women of Camp CADI—past, present and future: you are all amazing, strong and courageous.

To all Childhood Sexual Abuse survivors.

To my Wise Woman for inspiration, support, believing in me, caring and "teaching" me the most important lesson of all about finding my authentic self. Thank-you, I love you.

Acknowledgments

My daughters: Ashleigh, Felicia and Rebecca—thank you for your patience while I re-invented myself. You are amazing young women. I am very proud of you and I love you.

To all the strong women in my life: Diane, Barb, D.Z., J.C., J.S., Rivka, Sharon, Wanda… thank-you.

To my publisher: thank-you for taking on projects that nobody else wants to touch and knowing that these are important topics.

Preface

If you are picking up this book, maybe you are a survivor or maybe you care about one. *101 Tips For Survivors of Sexual Abuse* is the book I wish I had when I started my journey. I just wanted to know if what I was experiencing was "normal."

Let me assure you, there is no "normal," but instead all feelings are acceptable. As you flip through the book, you'll probably notice that the tips aren't grouped under headings like "self-esteem" or "managing anger". This was a deliberate design because, as I found out, healing is a messy affair. It does not come in neat little categories.

Healing is highly unpredictable. The range of emotions that you will go through changes rapidly. Just go with the flow and be gentle on yourself. Remember, there is no timetable and there is no right or wrong way to heal. These are the key messages of this book!

The journey will be hard but well worth the trouble. Each of you has the power to heal and live a wonderful life.

Wishing you courage on your journey...

Amy Barth,
May 2009

Foreword

101 Tips For Survivors Of Sexual Abuse reaches out as a helping hand to survivors. In 38 years as a therapist with a specialty in treating abuse and trauma, I have witnessed the denial, even by professionals, that sexual abuse occurs. Professionals as well as the general public are now more informed about the existence of sexual abuse, but sadly, I am still shocked by the continued avoidance of dealing with sexual abuse. Learning about this injustice and taking action to prevent and treat its damaging effects remains a commitment to be embraced by everyone. Knowledge is strength. You need to know, *most* importantly that you are not alone, others care about you, we can all face the problem of sexual abuse, and there is healing.

In this process of healing there are times when even the most informative material is too burdensome. Amy Barth's *101 Tips* can be a beginning place to take hold, an anchor to slow the overwhelming feelings of powerlessness, and a bridge to a new life of being who you really are.

You can read and reread the Tips. As you feel safer and stronger, you can put them into practice by doing some of the suggested activities. You will come up with even more effective and creative ways to make them work in your own life. If you are seeing a therapist, you can share the Tips with him or her and use them as a guide to document just exactly how you are taking hold and bringing about change in your life. Your growth and healing is no longer in *any way* connected to your abuser.

Once you are safe, YOU can be in charge of your happiness.

Karen R. Nash, LCSW

How to Use this Book

- Highlight the tips that resonate with you, so that you can find them quickly, when you need them.
- Please make this your mantra and say it everyday: "It wasn't my fault and I can heal."
- You can turn any tip into an affirmation. An affirmation is a declaration that something is *true*. Affirmations should avoid negations such as "don't" or "not". Rewrite them in positive language only.
- Post affirmations on your mirror, in your locker, in any private space that is your own.
- Sometimes a tip will bring up resistance, emotions, or unexplained tears. Try journaling about your feelings and reactions when embracing a challenging tip.

101 Tips

1. "It wasn't my fault." Make it your mantra and say it every day until you believe it.

2. Forgive yourself.

3. Trust yourself.

4. There is not a timetable for healing.

5. Healing can take a lifetime.

6. It does get better.

7. Listen to your truth.

8. Sexual abuse does not define who you are. It happened to you, but it definitely does not define you.

9. Take care of yourself.

10. Feel your feelings.

11. There is no reason for you to be ashamed.

12. You don't need to feel guilty.

13. You don't need to prove anything to anybody.

14. You're not a failure.

15. You didn't do anything to cause it. It was your perpetrator's fault.

16. Cry, if you want to.

17. Live in your body: Respect it, Move it, *Love* it.

18. Don't numb your feelings with: food, drugs, alcohol, shopping, cutting, sex, TV, shoplifting, or thrill seeking.

19. Ask for help if you need it and realize there is no shame in that.

20. Find a therapist (make sure you click, if not it won't help).

21. Choose relationships wisely.

22. If you are feeling needy, don't make up stories to get your needs met. It will hurt relationships in the future.

23. Breathe!

24. Learn to trust others: do it in baby steps.

25. Find healthy coping mechanisms: art, dance, music, be creative , exercise, journaling, yoga, meditation. These are just a few...

26. Laugh!

27. Nurture yourself or ask for nurturing.

28. Pamper yourself during the hard times.

29. Connect with others.

30. Love yourself!

31. Things to do when your angry: throw eggs at trees, punch a pillow, paint, scream, talk to a friend, breathe.

32. Get rid of self defeating talk.

33. Say nice things to yourself.

34. Trust your instincts.

35. Join a support group.

36. Read. There is a wealth of good info available.

37. Remember, you are not alone.

38. Accept that certain things may continue to trigger you.

39. Don't let fear hold you back.

40. Keep a gratitude journal.

41 Don't be silent about what happened. Share your story.

42. Volunteer with groups that are dedicated to Breaking the Silence.

43. Be open to processing new ways to see things.

44. Listen to your gut feeling.

45. Never blame yourself.

46. If you've never told, go ahead and tell, It's your right and please don't worry what other people will think.

47. Learn to soothe yourself.

48. Ask for hugs from friends.

49. Figure out what makes you feel safe.

50. Have an emergency kit for the tough times. Some ideas: phone #s of people you can reach out to, soothing tea, chocolate, art supplies, a funny movie or anything you think might help.

51. Be yourself! (find your authentic self)

52. Allow yourself to be happy.

53. Accept all feelings.

54. Recognize that your body did not betray you, your perpetrator did.

55. Don't feel guilty if your body responded. Bodies respond when they are stimulated. It does not mean you enjoyed it!

56. You could not have stopped it.

57. Abuse is about power and control.

58. You will have flashbacks.

59. It's normal to have suicidal thoughts, but please don't act on them. (if you are feeling this way, please call a hotline or find someone you can talk too).

60. It takes courage to heal.

61. Expect that it is going to be emotionally painful when you begin healing.

62. You are going to have to be vulnerable.

63. It's OK to be angry.

64. Have compassion for yourself.

65. You have a right to say "No".

66. You will get to a point where the memories are not so intrusive.

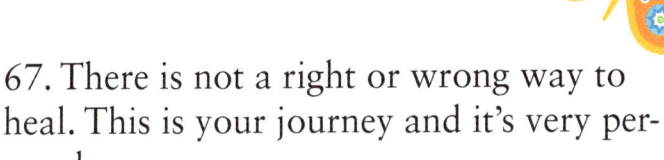

67. There is not a right or wrong way to heal. This is your journey and it's very personal.

68. Find ways to build your self-esteem.

69. Accept your body for where it is now.

70. People will believe you.

71. You matter.

72. You are a survivor!

73 Hang in there.

74. You are not bad.

75. Don't listen when people tell you to "just get over it."

76. You don't have to stay in an abusive relationship. It may feel familiar, but you deserve better.

77. You are worthy of friends, love and happiness.

78. Believe in yourself.

79. Recognize your self-destructive behaviors and make an effort to change them.

80. Recognize your need to control situations.

81. Let your defenses down.

82. Be open to new experiences.

83. It's up to you whether you want to confront your perpetrator. (If you want to do so, talk it over with someone first and weigh the pros and cons)

84. You may have panic attacks.

85. You can take your power back.

86. Be kind to the child within (don't punish that child any more).

87. Listen to your inner voice.

88. You don't have to stay stuck.

89. Don't worry if you feel "needy" when you start to heal. It's OK and eventually you won't feel that way anymore.

90. Have patience with yourself.

91. Watch your tendency to want to over-achieve to prove that you are OK.

92. You are not inadequate.

93. Don't be afraid to fail, everybody does!

94. Don't be afraid of the journey, It can be very hard but it is definitely worth it.

95. Healing hurts.

96. It does help to talk.

97. Don't be afraid to admit to what you are feeling because you are afraid of what other people will think. Feelings aren't right or wrong. They just are...

98. Take your time.

99. Adopt healthy coping mechanisms.

100. There is not *one* right way to define healing. Healing looks different to everybody!

101. REMEMBER: IT WAS NOT YOUR FAULT...

Things to do when having a "bad moment"
- Take ten deep, cleansing breaths
- Listen to a guided imagery CD
- Call a friend
- Email a friend
- Watch your favorite comedy
- Laugh
- Sing

These are just some ideas. The possibilities are endless, but you should make a list *before* you are having a bad moment. This way you will have resources that can help you get through that time. Consider getting a box and filling it with different art supplies and projects that you work on during the difficult times.

Exercises to Strengthen Your Core

1. List your core beliefs about yourself and see how they change over time...

2. List the different ways you can take care of yourself.

3. Try something new every day.

4. Be open to trying new ways to process things and observe how other people process things.

5. Journal how you feel each day.

6. Journal about what your inner voice is saying to you.

7. Journal about your self-defeating talk. Listen to what *you* are saying and replace it with positive talk!

8. Do a collage that represents your feelings.

9. What does courage mean to you? Can you draw what it looks like or write about it? Try different forms of art.

10. Make a collage of the strong people in your life that you can turn to during tough times.

11. Burn a CD of the music that makes you feel happy for those tough times.

12. How do you picture healing? See how many different ways you can express it and see if it changes over time...

Come up with your own activities and add to the list...

Bibliography / Suggested Reading

Davis, L. (1991). *Allies in healing: When the person you love was sexually abused as a child.* New York, N.Y.: HarperPerennial.

This book focuses on the partners of women sexually abused as children, who are living with the consequences of this abuse. It is written in a question and answer format, dealing with such topics as intimacy, family issues and realistic expectations. Also included are stories of eight couples and their struggles and successes.

Bass, E., & Davis, L. (1988). *The courage to heal: A guide for women survivors of child sexual abuse.* New York: Perennial Library.

This book is a classic resource for women who were sexually abused as children. Clearly written and filled with writing exercises and self-assessments, it is a reliable guide to the healing process from childhood sexual abuse. Many survivors' stories are woven into the text.

Davis, L. (1990). *The courage to heal workbook: For women and men survivors of child sexual abuse.* New York: Perennial Library.

This is an inspiring book for all women healing from the effects of child sexual abuse. It is in a workbook format, and includes checklists, writing and art projects, open-ended questions and activities which serve to guide the survivor through the healing process.

Feuereisen, P., & Pincus, C. (2005). *Invisible girls: The truth about sexual abuse*. Emeryville, CA: Seal Press.

Invisible Girls weaves together powerful first-person narratives with gentle guidance and seasoned insights to help girls through the maze of feelings that swirl around abuse.

About the Author

Amy Barth is a thriver. Her background is in social work and she founded the non-profit *Safe Girls Strong Girls* in 2005. SGSG is committed to breaking the silence of Childhood Sexual Abuse (CSA) and giving girls their voices back. One project of SGSG is Camp CADI, a one-of-a-kind camp where girls can heal and just be girls again.

Amy is the author of several books including *Annabelle's Secret*. Amy lives near Atlanta, Georgia with her husband and has three college-age daughters.

Amy's website is **www.AmyJBarth.com**